What causes acid rain?

First published in Great Britain by Heinemann Library
an imprint of Heinemann Publishers (Oxford) Ltd
Halley Court, Jordan Hill, Oxford OX2 8EJ

OXFORD LONDON EDINBURGH MADRID
ATHENS BOLOGNA PARIS MELBOURNE
SYDNEY AUCKLAND SINGAPORE TOKYO
IBADAN NAIROBI HARARE GABORONE
PORTSMOUTH NH (USA)

98 97 96 95 94

10 9 8 7 6 5 4 3 2 1

British Library Cataloguing in Publication Data is available from the British Library on request.

ISBN 0 431 07642 1

Cover designed and pages typeset by Philip Parkhouse
Printed in China

Picture Credits
pp. 2-3, Kurt Carloni/Artisan, 1991; pp. 4-5, © Bruce Davidson/Survival Anglia; pp. 6-7, Kurt Carloni/Artisan, 1991; pp. 8-9, © Gareth Stevens, Inc., 1991/Ken Novak; pp. 10-11, Kurt Carloni/Artisan, 1991; pp 12-13, © Bill Bachman/NHPA; pp. 14-15, © RHPL/Picture Perfect USA; pp. 16-17, © Phil Degginger/Picture Perfect USA; pp. 18-19, © 1992 Greg Vaughn; pp. 20-21, © Mark Edwards/Still Pictures; pp. 22-23, © L. Linkhart/Visuals Unlimited; p. 24, © L. Linkhart/Visuals Unlimited

Cover photograph © Science Photo Library/Simon Fraser
Back cover photograph © Sygma/D. Kirkland

Series editor: Elizabeth Kaplan
Series designer: Sabine Beaupré
Picture researcher: Diane Laska
Consulting editor: Matthew Groshek

Contents

Words that appear in the glossary are printed in **bold** the first time they occur in the text.

Exploring our environment

Look around you. You see forests, fields, lakes and rivers. You see farms, factories, houses and cities. All these things make up our **environment**. Sometimes there are problems with the environment. For example, **acid rain** pollutes lakes and rivers and kills animals that live in them. It destroys forests and drives away the wildlife. What is acid rain? How does it differ from ordinary rain? Let's find out.

How is the Earth's water recycled?

Rain is water that falls from clouds in the sky. The Sun **evaporates** water from the oceans, lakes and rivers. The water **vapour** rises and forms clouds high above us. Eventually the water in the clouds falls as rain.

There is only a certain amount of water on Earth. This water evaporates and falls as rain over and over again. The process that causes rain to form, fall and evaporate is called the **water cycle**. The water cycle recycles the Earth's water in a natural way.

What are acids?

Acids are sour liquids found in many living things. Lemons taste sour because they contain an acid. Spinach leaves and tomatoes also contain acids. There are even acids in your stomach.

8

Ordinary rain contains only a tiny amount of acid. But acid rain is rain that has become polluted. This polluted rain can be as acidic as vinegar or lemon juice.

9

How does rain become acidic?

As rain falls to the ground, it mixes with gases in the **atmosphere**. Some of the gases contain the elements **sulphur** and **nitrogen**. When these gases mix with water, acids form. This is how rainwater becomes acidic.

Long ago, acid rain was not a problem. Only in recent years has the rain become acidic. This is because the air is more polluted than it used to be. Air pollution causes acid rain.

11

The pollution problem

In many places you can see how polluted the
air is. Look out over a large city on a hot
summer's day. You will probably see a
brown hazy layer floating above the horizon.
This mixture of smoke, dust and gases is
called **smog**. In some cities, smog hangs in
the air for days at a time.

Burning too much coal, oil and petrol causes
smog. The smoke from burning these fuels
contains sulphur and nitrogen gases which
cause acid rain.

12

What does acid rain destroy?

Acid rain dissolves many types of rock. It discolours stone buildings, eats away marble statues and ruins structures which have stood for centuries.

Acid rain falls into lakes and rivers. The acidic water kills many fish. Frogs, newts, worms and insects may also die.

Acid rain falls over forests and soaks down into the soil. Some trees cannot live in the acidic soil. Entire forests may be wiped out.

Where does acid rain fall?

Acid rain falls all over the world. This is because winds scatter the gases that cause acid rain over all parts of the globe, so acid rain can form anywhere.

On the tops of mountains in New England in the United States, in the forests of eastern Canada and in other places far from cities, towns and factories, acid rain takes its toll. In fact, some of the world's most remote and beautiful places have problems with acid rain.

How can acid rain be stopped?

The best way to stop acid rain is to stop polluting the air with the sulphur and nitrogen gases that cause acid rain. Coal can have its sulphur removed before it is burned. The smoke that factories give off can also be cleaned. Devices called **scrubbers** remove sulphur gases from smoke.

Nitrogen gases are much harder to clean from the air. These gases form mainly in car and lorry **exhausts**. Scientists are working on ways to cut down on these nitrogen gases.

What can you do?

Power stations and cars are the biggest sources of sulphur and nitrogen gases. You can help prevent acid rain by using less electricity and by finding other ways to get about other than by car. Turn off lights when you leave a room. Ask your parents to turn down the electric fire or central heating. Walk or cycle instead of going by car.

Some trees take the acid out of acid rain. Planting and caring for these trees is another way to help solve the problem of acid rain.

A cleaner, greener world

The problem of acid rain cannot be solved overnight. It will take a long time to find clean sources of energy to replace coal, oil and petrol. But every little thing each person can do to reduce pollution will help. Look around you. Look for ways in which you can make your world a cleaner, greener place.

22

Glossary

acid: a sour liquid; strong acids can burn the skin

acid rain: rain that has become acidic by mixing with certain gases in the atmosphere

atmosphere: the gases that surround the Earth

environment: the natural and artificial things that make up our surroundings

evaporate: to change from a liquid to a gas

exhaust: the gases given off by cars, lorries and other motor vehicles

nitrogen: a chemical element which, in its gaseous state, contributes to acid rain

pollution: the addition of harmful dust, liquids or gases to the environment

scrubbers: devices that clean sulphur and other pollutants out of factory smoke before the smoke is released into the air

smog: a type of air pollution which forms from a mixture of smoke, dust and gases

sulphur: a chemical element which, in its gaseous state, contributes to acid rain

vapour: a gas that floats in the air

water cycle: the process by which rain forms, falls and evaporates on Earth

Index